The Power Of LinkedIn

The #1 Guide to LINK & GROW your Business

www.SydneyWebConsultants.com.au

Sue Kennedy

First Printing, 2013

Printed in the United States of America

Income Disclaimer

This book contains business strategies, marketing methods and other business advice that, regardless of my own results and experience, may not produce the same results (or any results) for you. I make absolutely no guarantee, expressed or implied, that by following the advice below you will make any money or improve current profits, as there are several factors and variables that come into play regarding any given business.

Primarily, results will depend on the nature of the product or business model, the conditions of the marketplace, the experience of the individual, and situations and elements that are beyond your control.

As with any business endeavor, you assume all risk related to investment and money based on your own discretion and at your own potential expense.

Liability Disclaimer

By reading this book, you assume all risks associated with using the advice given below, with a full understanding that you, solely, are responsible for anything that may occur as a result of putting this information into action in any way, and regardless of your interpretation of the advice.

You further agree that our company cannot be held responsible in any way for the success or failure of your business as a result of the information presented below. It is your responsibility to conduct your own due diligence regarding the safe and successful operation of your business if you intend to apply any of our information in any way to your business operations.

Terms of Use

The Power Of LinkedIn

The #1 Guide to LINK & GROW your Business

Table of Contents

INTRODUCTION

SydneyWeb Consultants
Recession Proof Marketing

"Good business leaders create a vision, articulate the vision, passionately own the vision, and relentlessly drive it to completion"
- Jack Welch

The training in this book will take you through the process of setting up your LinkedIn account and creating your profile. Plus we will show you several ways that you can use LinkedIn to expand and grow your business.

LinkedIn is the largest professional social network online today with an astounding 200+ million users and a targeted audience of business professionals.

If you are a business professional and you do not have a powerful presence on LinkedIn, you are definitely missing out on valuable opportunities to connect and grow your business.

The training in this book will allow you to learn the process of developing your presence, build your network, market your business, market yourself, and measure your results.

LinkedIn enables you to network professionally, post and find jobs, and build thought leadership—while simultaneously helping the people you trust. A user can easily discover the people employed by a certain business, or the various businesses a certain person has worked for. But what makes LinkedIn truly different from other social media sites?

Take a look this analogy:

I am sure that you already know that every social media tool has its own personality. Facebook is a lot like the local hotel. A hotel is a place where you can go and chat with friends, tell a few jokes and relax a bit.

LinkedIn is more like a trade show—a place where you'd keep things pretty buttoned-up and formal, business like. No need to mention your vacation in Hawaii on LinkedIn. But that white paper, report or book you wrote? These are perfect for LinkedIn. So for these reasons alone, LinkedIn should be an integral part of your social media marketing.

Let's get started!

THE NEW AND IMPROVED LINKEDIN

"It is not the strongest of the species that survive, nor the most intelligent, but the one most responsive to change"
- Charles Darwin

While LinkedIn has been growing steadily since 2009 the actual 'face' of LinkedIn was not as inviting as other social media sites. At one time people who used LinkedIn were strictly business owners and professionals.

Now all of that has changed with the emergence of other social sites including Facebook and Google+. LinkedIn needed to make some changes to adapt to the popularity of people using these types of sites to make business connections.

Well 2012 was definitely the year that changed the look and feel of LinkedIn. If you log into your account today you are met with a larger profile picture with your latest job posted under your name. Next to this is listed your state or province and your current job title.

This larger profile page makes your entire page more inviting and easier to read. At the top of your profile page will be a news feed which combines a mixture of a Facebook news feed and a Twitter feed. Here you simply update your status or share a relevant link.

If you haven't used LinkedIn you may be surprised at how the site looks, compared to what you may have heard about them. With the increased use of social media it only makes sense for a company who at the end of 2012 had just reached 200 million members.

LinkedIn is still viewed as a professional social site that now makes connecting with other professionals that much easier.

Here is a quick overview of some of the changes that LinkedIn has made.

November 2012 – LinkedIn Events are no longer supported
January 2013 – LinkedIn Answers is no longer supported

June 2013 – LinkedIn Polls are no longer supported (Polls in Groups will be still supported)

Other changes that you will see are that you can add a bigger profile picture and that your number of recommendations is not shown at the top of your profile.

So whether you arc brand new to LinkedIn or haven't logged into your account in a long time, this training will navigate you through the new face of LinkedIn today!

GET CONNECTED WITH LINKEDIN

"A business has to be involving, it has to be fun, and it has to exercise your creative instincts"
- Richard Branson

When you first start your LinkedIn account, the free version is a great start. This is perfectly fine for developing good business connections within your market. Most likely you already have an account set up, if not just follow the basic directions to get one ready and then come back and follow the rest of this training.

LinkedIn suggests that having a completed profile provides you with a 40% greater chance for networking success, and they make it easy for you to understand how to achieve that 100% completion by following their tips and suggestions.

Having a completed profile is the most effective way to showcase all of who you are through your talents, background, experience, passions, interests, and areas of expertise. In addition, a completed profile is going to make you appear to be a more competent user in the network.

Your LinkedIn profile may be the first stop for a new introduction. With a solid foundation, you will be well positioned for the next phase, where you can grow your influence and build your business.

There is as mentioned above the free account on LinkedIn as well as three levels of a paid membership. The paid versions include Business, Business Plus and Executive. All three have monthly or annual payments.

The Business Plus is the level most recommended for businesses and to give you a quick overview the following are some of the features you can expect to get.

- Allows you to see 300 profiles
- Allows you to connect via LinkedIn in mail with responses guaranteed, 3 per month
- Look at profiles with premium search filters – 4 filters per month

- Provides you with the full profile of anyone in your network
- Provides you with the full list of who has viewed your profile

This is just a quick sampling of some of the upgraded features; you can view the full list once you have signed up for your free account.

Your free LinkedIn account will allow you to start making connections with other professionals in your market or niche.

Go to www.linkedin.com to sign up for your account.

The image below is your home page navigation bar, which we will refer to several times throughout this training. Just click on the home page tab anytime you are not sure where you are and then choose the relevant tab.

Setting Up Your Profile Page

Your profile on LinkedIn is extremely important. The words you use to describe your services and clients are used by LinkedIn as keywords. So by applying the correct terms in your profile you can show up high in the search results.

Please note that the search results for LinkedIn are based upon your connections. So while it is important to get a good number of connections, you don't want to start spamming people. This will not look good and only serve to get you into trouble with LinkedIn.

Before you can fully use LinkedIn as a business, you need to master LinkedIn as an individual user. While many people have an account, their profile is often incomplete, making it particularly useless. It is actually worse to have an incomplete profile as opposed to not having one at all.

Therefore, let us assume you already have some form of a LinkedIn profile (if not, go create one!), let's complete your profile so you can attain social media status and greatness.

To edit your profile page you will want to click on your **Profile** link and then click on the edit button. Your profile page will show up when anyone searches for you via the major search engines. If you do not wish this page to appear in any searches you can hide your profile by using the following method:

Move your cursor over the Profile link on the top of the page and then select edit.

Click the edit link that is located next to your profile URL and change the button next to where it says “make my public profile visible to no-one”.

Your LinkedIn profile will not appear in any search engines and will not be visible to anyone who is not a LinkedIn member. Please note that when you change your settings in this way it may take a few weeks to stop showing up in Internet searches.

The majority of people do want their profiles to display in the search engines, but if you have reasons why you would prefer not to, then just change this status. It can easily be changed back at any time.

Customising Your Profile URL

Go to settings and click on edit your public profile.

Click on Customise your public profile and add your chosen name. You just need to type in the last portion of the name you want to use here.

Note: Custom names are on a first come first served basis. They must be between 5 – 30 characters with no spaces, symbols or special characters of any kind.

LinkedIn will let you know if your chosen name is available or not. Select the closest variation if your first choice is not available.

Profile Settings

Once you are in your profile section you will see the following options:

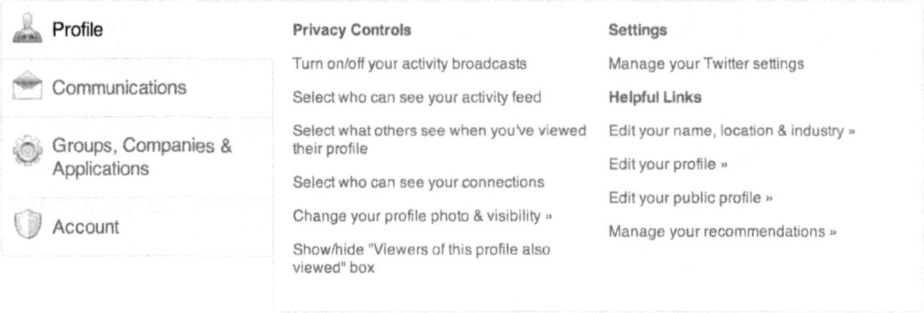

Here you can see what you can do inside this area. You can turn on or off your broadcasts. This controls your updates on your profile page.

Your activity feed controls who can see your activity and you can set this to everyone, your network, your connections or for only you.

The **select what others see** is how someone else will see your profile. You can set this to display your name and headline, or to be anonymous and show your industry and job title or you can choose to be totally anonymous.

Under settings you can add your Twitter link. Be sure to connect your Twitter and LinkedIn accounts together. This way when you update your status it will automatically be tweeted for you.

It is a good idea to use the status feature as much as possible. You can simply state that you are working on a clients website, or creating a new product or writing a new article or report. It just shows people that you are actively using your profile.

The other sections include editing your name and location as well as industry. The main section you will want to go into is thc "Edit your profile" area. In this section you will see different areas where you can add relevant information that you want people to see.

- Background
- Experience
- Publications
- Skills & Expertise
- Education
- Additional Info – includes interests, personal details and contact advice
- Honors & Awards
- Organisations
- Recommendations

- Connections
- Groups
- Following

Make sure you fill out all of these areas in as much detail as possible. In the Skills & Expertise section highlight the skills that you are trying to promote. For a graphic designer this would include adding information about how long you have been a designer and the areas that you really excel at. If your expertise is in creating websites or book covers and graphics then highlight these factors.

If you were an offline consultant or coach then include this in as many of the sections as possible. The Additional Info area is great for adding how a client can contact you as well as including your website address. Again feature here the areas you excel at.

Select from the drop down menu "Edit Profile" link. Get ready to follow the 7 steps in setting up your profile effectively:

1. Include Full Name and Image.

Let's start with the very first section. This may sound like a no-brainer, but countless LinkedIn users fail to include their full name and picture. Display your first and last name to ensure people can find you. Using a first name with a last initial is not sufficient—especially when a prospective client or employer is trying to locate your profile. Then, upload an image. Research suggests that profiles without photos are rarely viewed, as they are perceived as profiles not in use or spammers.

2. Personalise Your Headline.

Customise your "Professional Headline," which will automatically update in the future as your current position. However, you have the option of altering it to something else, which may be more appealing to prospective clients or employers. But keep in mind that if a client were seeking you out on LinkedIn, it would be helpful to include your current position in the headline. In general, keep it short and sweet. You only have 120 characters at the top of your profile to describe what you do to the world and grab their attention. Use brief, descriptive, compelling keywords so the right professionals on LinkedIn can discover you.

TIP: If you switch jobs, your professional headline will reflect that. So instead of trying to recall what your perfect headline was, have it saved for easy accessibility.

3. Add Work History.

Click on the "Experience" section. At the very

minimum you should list your most recent positions. Fill out the information about that job. If your company appears in the drop down once you start typing, click on it to ensure you get grouped with fellow employees under company searches.

TIP: Avoid adding the various positions you held in the many organisations, clubs, and/or societies at your school (whether you are currently in school or 10 years removed). While these are all great experiences, if you want to tailor your profile to a professional environment, highlight only your professional experience—internships, jobs, etc. LinkedIn was wise enough to know how to weigh the clout of each type of work, by including a section under education to separately list these activities.

4. Complete the "Summary" section of your profile:

This is your chance to really describe who you are and how you help people. I recommend that you write your summary in the third person. Otherwise, you'll be using the letter "I" quite a bit, which can be off-putting.

5. Complete the "Skills & Expertise" section of your profile

Utilise customer-focused keywords, as these are

the terms that will help you show up in search results within LinkedIn. When thinking about these keywords, brainstorm words and phrases that people in your target markets might search for to find someone with your background, experience, and service offering.

6, Complete the "Interests" and "Groups and Associations" sections

Each of these terms will be hyper-linked and will take you to other users in the network who share these interests.

7. Customise Your LinkedIn URL.

You'll want to create a personalised LinkedIn URL. Still under the "Edit Profile" page, look at the bottom of your profile image. You'll see a line that shows your linkedIn address with an "Edit" link next to it. From there, you'll be taken to a new screen. Scroll down and to the right of the page you'll see where it says "Your Public Profile URL", under "Your current URL" you will see a link that says "Customise your public profile URL" – click on this to create your customised LinkedIn URL quickly and easily.

TIP: Try to avoid using your company name in your LinkedIn URL. After all, there are no guarantees you'll be at that company forever.

8. Customise your Website URL's.

Website URL's are just as important as your customer LinkedIn URL. Click edit next to "Additional Information." Here you can include your interests, groups and associations, and any honors and awards. Each is self-explanatory. However, the first section calls for websites. The drop down menu for adding a website lists options such as Personal Website, Company Website, Blog, etc. We recommend choosing "Other"— regardless of what kind of site it is. This will allow you to insert your own Title, so instead of a hyperlinked word that says "Blog," it will be more specific, such as "Marketing Blog."

9. Ask for Recommendations.

You'll notice a hyperlink under each position that says, "Ask for recommendations." A recommendation can help to distinguish a traditional position by illustrating how well you performed through a colleague's narrative.

TIP: When requesting a recommendation, do not simply send the generic message LinkedIn creates for you. Include some specific projects you worked on so that your recommender remembers the particular work you did and speak to it. Notice the difference between: "Pete was a creative thinker who got the job done", and "Pete created and implemented a blogging strategy that helped generate 163 leads in one weeks time."

10. Give recommendations first

Request recommendations that can be displayed on your profile. The best way to receive recommendations is to first give them!

Hint: You will need at least three recommendations in order for LinkedIn to label your profile "completed."

11. Connect Your Twitter Account with LinkedIn.

Go to Profile Settings (where your name is), click on the link that reads, "Manage your Twitter settings". Click edit to manage your Twitter settings. Not only should you display your Twitter handle, but you should share tweets as well. Your tweets are one of the only ways to make your profile personable and not focused solely around your professional life. A client or employer will want to see how you speak and think in addition to the more traditional information available on your resume.

TIP: Select the option to only share tweets that contain a LinkedIn hashtag (#in or #li). This will allow you to filter, which tweets appear on your profile. This way, if you tweet about seeing someone walk into a door while drunk, it'll get buried away in your Twitter stream and you can focus on sharing more professional tweets. Keep in mind that not all LinkedIn users are updating their accounts as often as Twitter users, so having a filter can avoid spamming your connections.

12. Grow Your Network.

You now have enough information on your profile to start growing your network! Just go to the upper right hand side of the menu bar and click on the link that says Interests. Scroll down to Groups. Then type in a subject you're interested in (e.g., marketing, sales, real estate, etc.). You'll notice that when you do a search, LinkedIn provides suggestions not only on "Groups" but also in several other categories such as People, Jobs, and Companies.

Don't be shy about reaching out to organisations or people on LinkedIn. That's what it's for. But avoid doing a bunch of outreach all at once because people will pick up on the spammy nature of it. Just pretend you're at a party and reach out to people one at a time. That way, you'll come across as more genuine and sincere.

Your Home Page

Your **Home** page is different to your profile page and you don't want to confuse the two.

Your profile page will display your photo along with your activity, background etc. Your home page is the page you want to use to update your status each day. This is the page that works in a similar fashion to a Facebook page.

Basically you update your status by including a short paragraph on what you have done or you can include links to your own articles or other news related items. Just as you would when you share things you like on other social sites.

The image above shows you what your home page will look likc, your photo will appear on the left hand side.

Directly underneath you will see that **LinkedIn Today** has recommendations for you. Then below this is the area where all of your connections have updated their status recently.

This area will show you things like who has just commented on a group discussion. Who has just updated their book or who has made connections etc?

This newsfeed will also show you who have joined which groups on LinkedIn. This could potentially be extremely useful if you are looking to build relationships within a certain niche or business area. You can also join the same groups.

Underneath each section is a comments field where you can join in the conversation. This area can be used to add general comments but you can also use it to add your own useful tips, insights and expertise.

On the right hand side of your home page you will see that LinkedIn suggests a '**People You May Know**' section. These are simply suggestions of people that have the same interests as you or who may be in the same business arena. If you wish to connect with them you simply click on the button and fill out the invitation.

The '**Who's Viewed Your Profile**' box allows you to see how many people have looked at your profile page over the last 90 days. Plus it tells you how many times you have shown up in searches in the past 15 days. This is useful information and if you are not showing up in searches you can adjust some of the keywords you entered in your profile to increase this.

The next area **'Your LinkedIn Network'** shows you how many connections you have and how many people are in your extended network. This number includes those people who are connected with your first three levels of connections.

Other areas that show up on your home page include **Jobs You May be Interested in** and **Groups You May Like** along with **Companies You May Want to Follow**.

Skills & Expertise

The Skills & Expertise area, which is now included in LinkedIn is a new feature, which was recently added. This feature is proving to be extremely popular and could be compared to Liking someone on Facebook or repining an image on Pinterest.

The way this works is you add the 'skills' that you feel you offer to employers and clients. Then people in your network can endorse you as well. To endorse someone you must be on their profile page and then hover your mouse over the endorsement. You then click to endorse and the person will receive an email notification that you have just endorsed them.

This is a great way to show someone that you are still around, a reminder of sorts. Plus by endorsing someone you are showing him or her that you appreciate his or her work.

When you search for a person on LinkedIn this is a screenshot of what you will see:

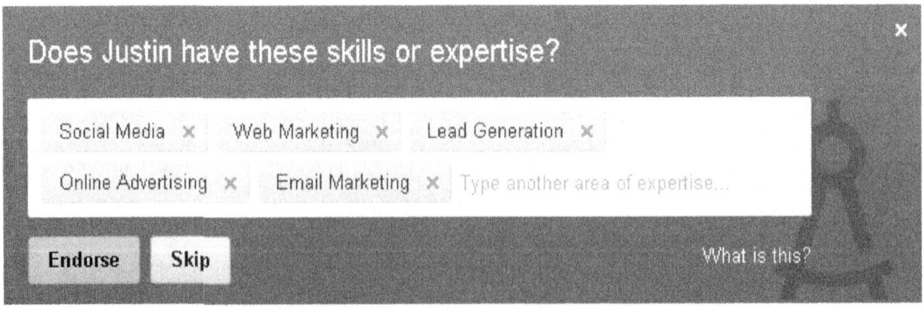

You can add more tags or remove ones and then click on the Endorse button. This will bring up other people in your network with similar tags. You can endorse these people as well or just skip the section.

The person who was just endorsed will receive an email that states the person's name and invites you to see all of your endorsements. Of course it would be great for you to endorse that person back!

This is an extremely quick way to show a person that you are active on LinkedIn and can act as a reminder that you are part of their network. This is proving to be an interactive and fun part of using LinkedIn.

HOW TO USE LINKEDIN EFFECTIVELY

"In business, I have discovered that my purpose is to do my best to my utmost ability every day. That is my standard. I learned early in my life that I had high standards"
- Donald Trump

Once you have set up your account and filled out your profile, you must be wondering what is your next step? Like any social site you want to start interacting with people. One of the easiest ways to do this is by joining **LinkedIn Groups**.

Before you go ahead and start joining them, think about the type of groups that would be beneficial to you. What type of people are you looking to connect with? Are you using LinkedIn primarily to find work or to generate leads and contacts for your business?

If you want to promote your services and generate leads then look for LinkedIn Groups that could use what you have to offer. At the same time join groups related to your area of expertise. This way you can offer advice and tips to people, plus this will help build a solid relationship and brand you as a professional.

As we mentioned before LinkedIn will automatically recommend groups for you on your home page. These recommendations are based on how you filled out your profile information. So this area is a good place to start when searching for suitable groups.

To search for groups on LinkedIn go to the top of your home page and click on Interests. There will be a drop down box with the following recommendations:

- Companies
- Groups
- Influencers

The Create a Group (located up the top of the page in the middle) is a good feature if you cannot find any suitable groups to join, or if you want to start your own group on LinkedIn. This might be a great option for starting a local business network or for a creating a specific niche group.

Remember, if you create your own LinkedIn group you must be prepared to monitor and lead the group on a daily basis. This could be another great way to show people how to use your product or service to enhance their business. You don't want to just sell yourself in this group. Give out advice and be helpful to others, this will again help strengthen your position as a leader within your industry.

The one huge benefit of creating a group is that it gives you access to an email broadcast tool for free. If used correctly this could be invaluable to your business.

The LinkedIn Group Directory is huge so you want to take some time to go through it to find suitable groups. Look for groups that have a good number of members and ones that are active.

With most groups you have to apply for membership within the group and will need to be approved first. This may be done quickly or it could take a few days. You will be notified by email once you are approved and then it is time to start getting active in your group.

It is important to not join too many groups at first; otherwise your entire day could be taken up with posting and commenting in the group. Instead it is recommended to just join a handful of groups first and then see what the group has to offer. If you are not receiving any valuable content or engagement then leave that particular group and join another.

When being active in the group it is wise to offer advice and helpful tips to other members. Provide them with answers to their questions and be sure to comment on their articles or other posts, which they make.

Only after you have been an active member in the group for a while is it a good idea to promote yourself or offer your services. Done the correct way this will look like a natural advancement and not blatant self-promotion.

Tips to promote your Group

1. Use other social media assets to promote your group

Promotion doesn't and shouldn't end with just LinkedIn members. Once you begin to strategically engage in social media, you need to optimise your own website for social media.

For the LinkedIn Group, it can be as simple as posting a logo and a link to your group in a prominent area of your website. In this way, your website visitors not only find out about your community, but they can also easily join it. If you have an email newsletter, don't forget to feature your group's logo there as well. An occasional tweet or Facebook post introducing your LinkedIn Group is another way to efficiently utilise social media to "advertise" your LinkedIn Group.

2. Keep LinkedIn group policies in mind

If you have ever been a member of a LinkedIn Group, you will know that many are filled with spammy link-building "discussions" that tarnish the atmosphere of the group and potentially the brand of the company sponsoring it. Social media marketing is really about relevance, so it is important to keep your group relevant by actively managing and keeping the irrelevant information out. Your first step in doing this is by creating a LinkedIn Group Policy.

LinkedIn has provided group managers with the ability to create a group policy under the title "Group Rules." It is here where you can set your expectations and rules for the group so that there is no misunderstandings with members should you need to remove them for posting spam. It is also a way to show your company's professional approach to managing the group, so I would recommend taking an extra step and customising the template that LinkedIn provides you in welcoming new members to either list the group rules or remind them to read them.

3. Create a LinkedIn group engagement strategy

Similar to how those who engage with your Facebook Page will help get your news noticed in each fan's personal news feed, engagement in your LinkedIn Group will be posted in members' network updates. So how does one foster group engagement?

When starting a group, you need to assume leadership by proactively starting conversations, posting relevant and timely news, and quickly reacting to the discussions and questions of others. This can be done in a time-effective manner by pre-scheduling some activities and utilising

LinkedIn's feature that allows group managers to receive updates about new discussions and comments the moment they happen. As membership grows, the discussions tend to become mostly self-generated, but it's still important to check the engagement volume on a regular basis and generate new discussions as needed.

There is no one-size-fits-all approach, but one tactic used by some group managers is to take an interesting discussion from another group. This could be completely repurposed if it is a general discussion.

If it is a discussion with unique content, it can be accredited to the person who started the discussion. A topic that generated a lot of discussion in a similar group is bound to be similarly successful in one's own group. Another idea? Discuss a recent blog post of yours.

LINKEDIN TODAY

"The only way to discover the limits of the possible is to go beyond them into the impossible"
- Arthur C. Clark

The LinkedIn Today feature is a customisable news feed provided on your home page. There are two ways to access this feature. If you are already logged into your account then simply click on the **News** tab on your home page bar. Otherwise view the page by visiting the following link: www.linkedin.com/today

While this feature cannot be removed from your home page it can be customised.

You can set your email frequency for receiving updates in your Settings Page under Email Preferences. Select from Daily, Weekly or No emails.

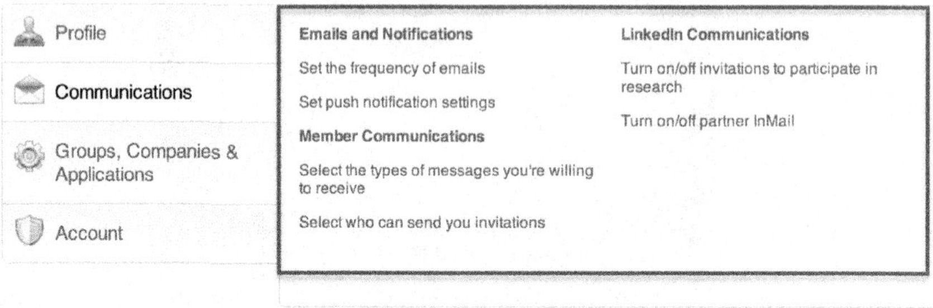

Just navigate through each setting and select your preferences.

To select news on specific industries and companies click on the News tab and then go to the gear icon on the top right hand side of your screen. You will be taken to the following screen:

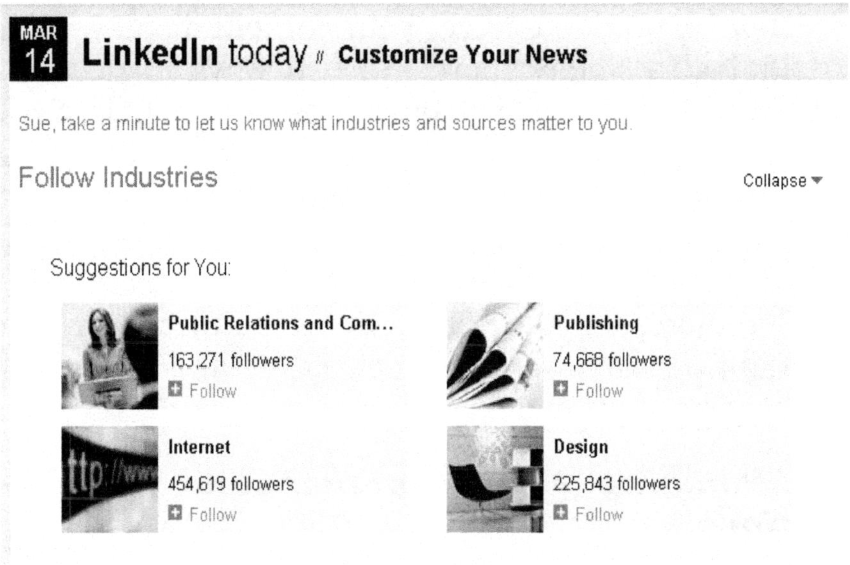

From the list provided to you click on Follow or click on Following to stop these feeds from showing. The text will change back to Follow.

How Does LinkedIn Today Choose What Content to Display

The news, which is displayed on LinkedIn Today, is taken from links and articles that are posted by members of LinkedIn. The company looks at what type of news is being shared by people and then sorts all of this information by Industry and by news source.

If a particular article is being shared rapidly then this will be given preference on the site.

If you would like to get your content displayed on LinkedIn Today there are two ways to do this. First provide a Share button on your article. Secondly you may contact the Business Development department at publisher@linkedin.com.

To increase your chances of getting seen on LinkedIn today share your content and allow it to be viewed publicly.

Managing Your Contacts and Connections

You can view all of your contacts by clicking on the **Network** tab of the home page navigation bar and then select "Contacts" from the dropdown menu.

It is possible for you to add labels to your contacts so that you can easily find them. These labels can be tags or done by company name, location as seen in the screenshot below.

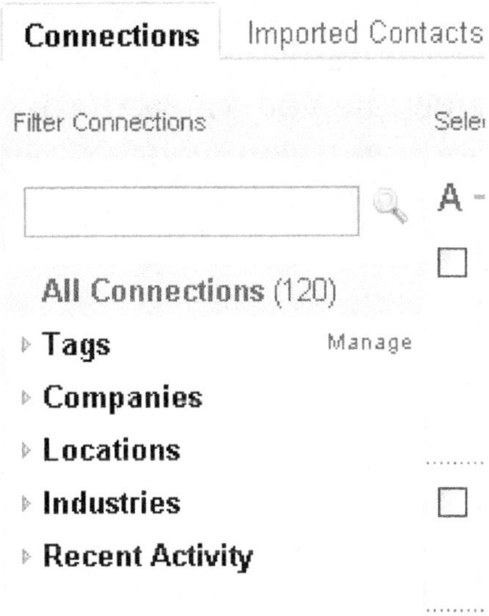

To organise your contacts add a checkmark to the box by the person's name and edit accordingly.

You can add additional contacts by clicking on Add Connections:

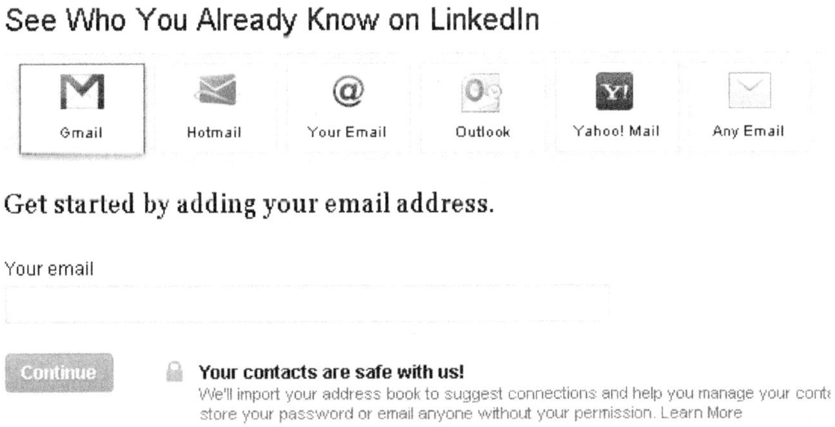

Add your email address and LinkedIn will search the various sources for people you know that are already on LinkedIn. Once your connections have been imported you can add them into your network.

FINDING A JOB ON LINKEDIN

"Believe in yourself and you will be un-stoppable"
- Emily Guay

It is easy to search for jobs on LinkedIn. Use the **Jobs** tab on your home page navigation and you will be taken to a new screen.

As you will see from the screenshot you can search for a job or post a job.

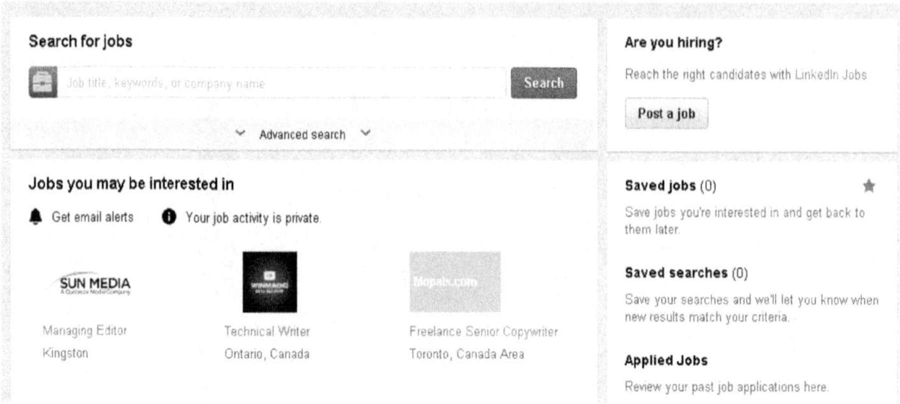

LinkedIn will automatically post jobs that you may be interested in as well. By scrolling down the page you will find jobs that are available in your network.

You can save selected jobs, save your searches and file your applications under applied jobs. All of this makes it easy to keep track of your job search.

There is a section called **Find Talent,** which is a paid service. This is primarily for employers to find the best candidates for their positions. By subscribing to this service, a company has the ability to unlock 100 additional names along with being able to email a selected number each month.

There are 3 levels to this subscription with each upgrade allowing you to search a higher number of people as well as being able to search within groups.

LinkedIn Companies

"The individual who wants to reach the top in business must appreciate the mighty force of habit and must understand that practices are what create habits. We must be quick to break those old habits that break us and hasten to adopt those practices that will become the habits that will help us achieve the success we desire"

- J. Paul Getty

The **Companies** tab is on your home page navigation bar under the "Interests" Tab and allows you to search all the companies in the LinkedIn directory.

Once you are following a company any updates will appear on this page as well. The right hand side will display a listing of recommendations of which companies to follow.

Adding Your Own Company

It is possible to get your own company listed in the LinkedIn directory? Yes, and to do this you need to click on the Add Company tab to get started.

You will need to verify that you own and run the company and will need to fill out the following confirmation page.

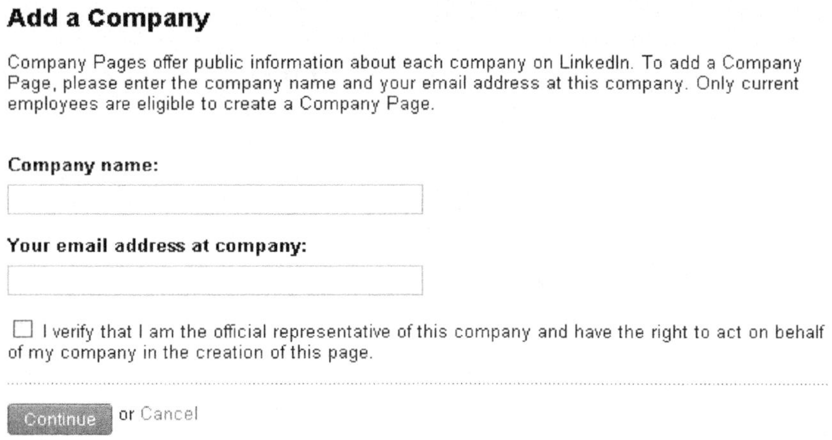

After submitting this form you will receive a confirmation email from LinkedIn, which will allow you to submit your company's details.

Your Company Page

Your company page looks like a mini website and is a great way to create additional interest for your product or service. Plus you can add several products, perfect if you publish reports or eBooks or just want to showcase different areas of your company.

This area has been improved in the recent LinkedIn updates and you can now add an image to your company page. The image must meet the following requirements:

- 646 x 220 – png, jpeg or gif with a maximum size of 2MB

To edit your company page click on the edit tab on the top right hand side and from here you will have the following options:

- Add your product or service
- View follower insights
- View page insights
- Add jobs
- Promote your page with LinkedIn ads

The add a product or service section allows you to include lots of information. You may include an image, choose from the available categories, write a brief description and include bullet points of your main features/benefits and you may include your product or website URL. Another nice feature is that you may include a YouTube video in this section, why not make this a promotional video?

Your company page also includes a contact page for use for anyone from LinkedIn. You can specify exactly who to contact for each product or service listing. This is a great feature that allows the right person to be contacted immediately. Technically each product you add can have different contact information.

The insights page provides you with useful information on how many followers you have and all of your recent activities in the past seven days.

This can provide you with full details on just who is following you, including what position they hold in the company and what industry they belong to. Click on each tab to display the relevant data.

Your page data includes information on how many page views you have received in the last seven days. Also included in this section are the number of unique visitors and how many page clicks you have received.

LinkedIn displays your followers' demographics, as shown in the following screenshot.

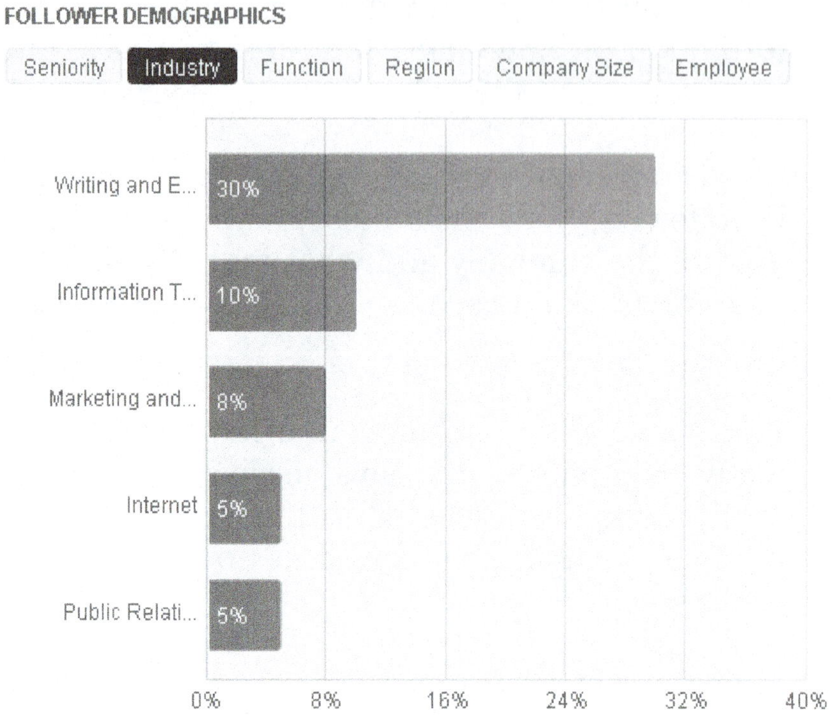

5 Steps To Complete Your Company Page

Now that your personal LinkedIn profile is top-notch, and you have a better understanding on why the heck you should have a LinkedIn company page, it's important to make that page blanketed with great information. A LinkedIn company page is the one page amidst those on your various social networks that calls for the most professionalism.

Just as a person profile is professional in its resume-like nature, yet has a touch of personality through Twitter streams and applications, a company page should emit a white-collar persona paired with some company character. With that in mind, here are 5 steps to complete your company page.

1. Include Basic Information. Go to "Companies" and select the "Add new company" link to the left of your screen. You will see a screen that asks you to fill in your company name and your email address. From there, LinkedIn will prompt you to fill in generic information about your company. Be sure to add a good description of what your company does, as this will be crucial in the user understanding what your company is all about.

2. Post Jobs. There is two ways to post jobs on the company page; first is the tab on the company page called "Careers", this is located to the right of the page, or secondly, you can click on the "Edit" button that is located on the top right hand side of your screen, from here, select "Add Jobs", you will be taken to a new page, click on the "Jobs" link. This feature allows you to post openings at your company. While your company may already have various methods of announcing that you're hiring, what better place to post a job opening than the very network where professionals live and explore? Let people know you're looking for new people to help build what is ultimately defined in your company description.

3. Include Products. Why not showcase what products your business has to offer? Click on the tab heading called "Products" on your company page, click on "Get Started".

You now have the option to "add a product, service, or other." Do it. LinkedIn will go through simple step-by-step instructions to help you broadcast these services.

4. Promote. The "Edit" button will show you a drop down; here you will find a link called "Promote your page with LinkedIn Ads" LinkedIn allows you to promote your company through an ad campaign. This feature is split into 4 simple steps, which LinkedIn takes you through in a very comprehensible manner. A "Common Questions" box also appears to the right of this page, so you can truly understand how the feature works. A LinkedIn ad campaign could help spread the word about your company as you build and integrate inbound marketing efforts into your business platform.

5. Measure Everything. Well, with everything provided on your company page, the fourth and final tab on your company page is "Insights." Remember that everything you do with Internet marketing involves taking the time to see how those efforts are playing out (this will help you determine whether or not those efforts are worth the time.) The "Insights" tab will allow you to

track page views and unique visitors on your overall page, as well as each individual tab. LinkedIn also measures how many clicks your products or services have received and the number of members following your company.

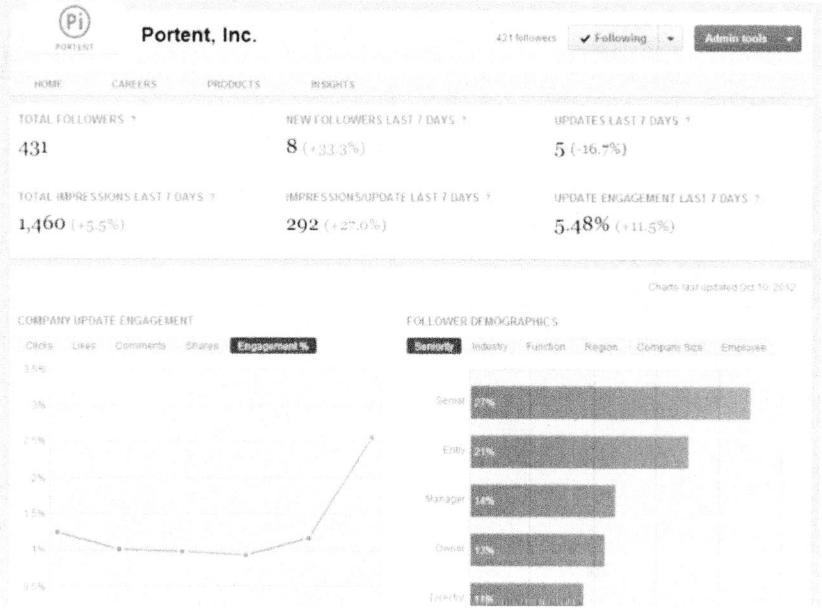

In addition, LinkedIn gives percentages for member visits. This tool can be helpful in understanding who your LinkedIn target audience is because the data is split into member visits by industry (marketing, finance, etc.), function (sales, research, etc.), and company (LinkedIn, etc.). You now have a wonderful company profile page—one that can be reached through your personal page. Now keep that momentum flowing as we head into the last step in perfecting your company page.

How To Turn On Company Status Updates

As mentioned earlier, a LinkedIn company page showcases all the people who currently work at that company. Anyone with a valid @companyname.com email address is able to edit the minimal information on the page. However, with the launch of LinkedIn's status update feature for these pages, only selected employees will be able to administrate. This will allow your company to have another platform to share information, and add some personality to your page (you need to broadcast your voice to become more personable!).

Here's a breakdown of the simple steps to activate status updates, which will appear on followers' LinkedIn homepages as well as the company's page itself. In addition, LinkedIn users can "Like," comment on, and share a company's updates, a la Facebook.

Visit your company page on linkedIn and you will see the following:

This is the company status update box that will allow you to share what is happening in your company!

THE INTERESTS TAB

"There's no shortage of remarkable ideas, what's missing is the will to execute them" - Seth Godin

The **Interests tab** is the final tab on your home page on the left hand side of the navigation bar.

This has a drop down menu, which includes the following choices:

- Companies

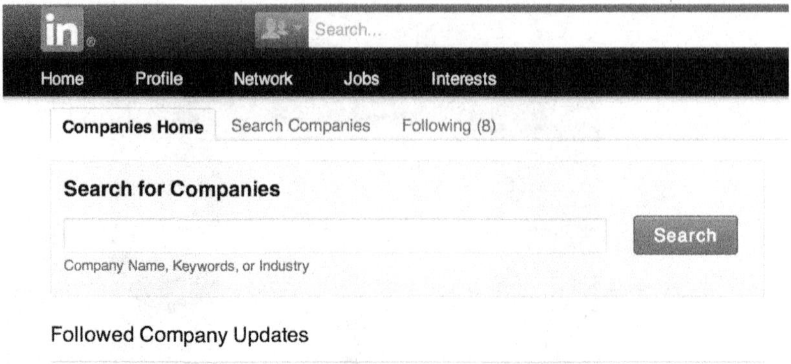

- # Groups

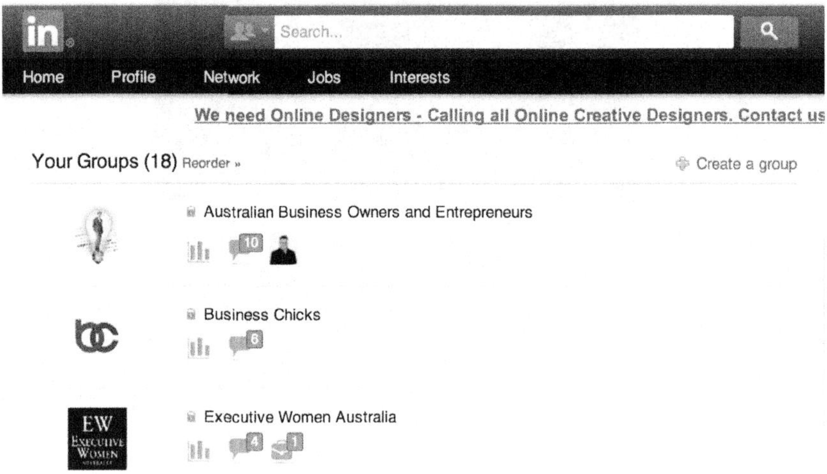

- # Influencers

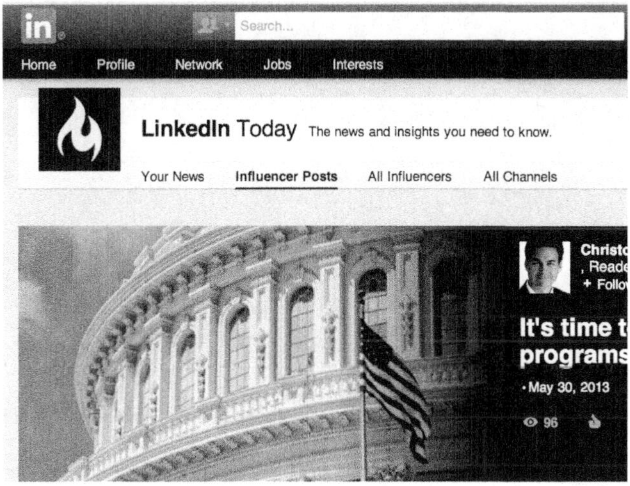

A description of each of these areas is included in the previous pages of this book.

THE PREMIUM SOLUTIONS TAB

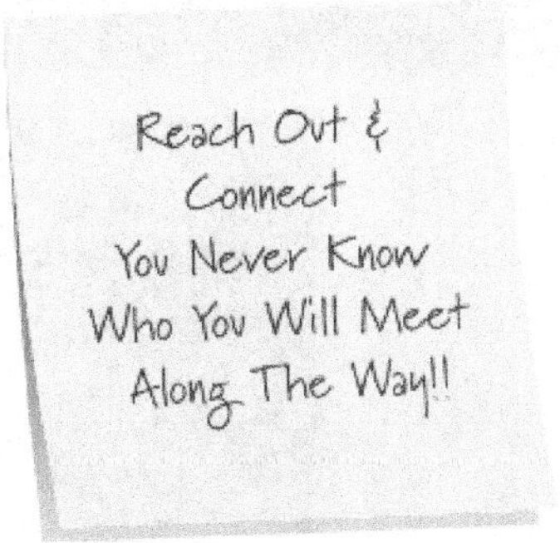

"The great accomplishments of man have resulted from the transmission of ideas of enthusiasm" - Thomas J. Watson

This tab has a drop down menu that includes:

- Post Job

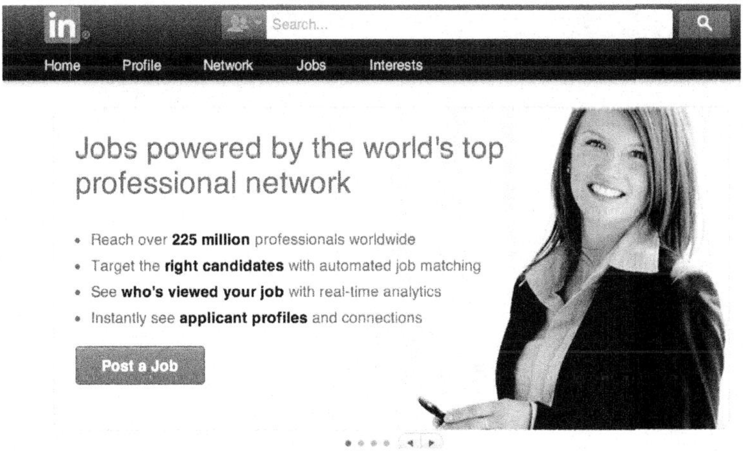

- Talent Solutions

- Advertise

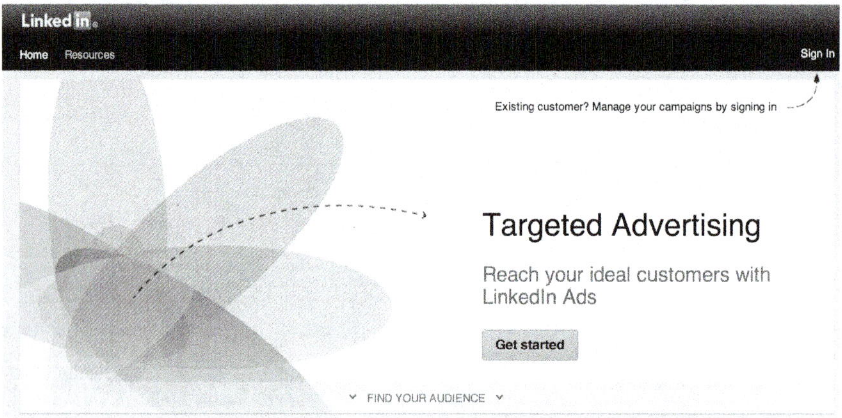

These sections allow you to find jobs, post jobs and advertise your business.

Connecting Twitter to LinkedIn

Don't forget to connect your Twitter account to LinkedIn. This way each time you post an update on your news feed it will automatically get re-tweeted. If you make the effort to post regularly on LinkedIn then you won't have to worry about logging in to your

Twitter account and finding topics to tweet about. It is a good idea to use the status feature as much as possible. You can simply state that you are working on a clients website, or creating a new product or writing a new article or report. It just shows people that you are actively using your profile.

NETWORKING WITH LINKEDIN

"Every accomplishment starts with a decision to try" - Unknown

How To Grow Your Network

Your first goal is to grow your connection list. One easy way is to join some Groups within LinkedIn as we mentioned earlier. As discussed, you can easily find groups within your industry to join, along with local groups. Also think about joining groups that could potentially use your services. If you offer coaching or graphic designs then look for groups that need these types of services.

The most powerful concept behind linkedIn is that it helps you find valuable people and informs you of the mutual connections you have with them, or your second and third degree networks. This really has enormous value. Why?

Well many people already have difficulty keeping track of all their first-degree contacts in their network. It is quite impossible to know whom our network knows. This is where LinkedIn keeps track of this for us, how awesome it that? Access to this information is extremely powerful.

So let's go over the steps on how to build a valuable network for you and your business.

How to get your Network started:

While there is true business opportunity within your second-degree network, you still need a first-degree network to be able to reach those second-degree connections. Here are three steps to build your first-degree network effectively and in a timely manner.

1. Connect with your direct, first degree network

Upload your contacts from Outlook, web mail like Hotmail, Gmail, Yahoo, AOL, or other address books. You can do this via the "Add Connections" tab (located under "Network"). Then you can log in to your email and find who has a profile on LinkedIn.

Look at the contacts, which are now available in "Imported Contacts" (under "Contacts" in the menu on the left). The people who are already on LinkedIn have a small blue icon with the letters "In." Since they are already using LinkedIn, they will be open for a connection with you. Select them.

Write a semi-personal message to them. First check, then "Add a personal note to your invitation." Then replace the standard "Hi, I'd like to add you to my network" message with something related to how you know them. You can't make it too personal when you use this method because you have selected several people.

2. Add previous colleagues and classmates to your network

While you are waiting for people to accept the invitations you sent, you can add more people to your network via a different method. Again, you are first focusing on the people who are already on LinkedIn because they will be more open to acccpt your invitation.

Use the tools LinkedIn provides for retrieving colleagues and classmates. Since LinkedIn works with the information in your profile, it is important that you already have completed the information about the companies you have worked for and the schools and universities you've attended.

Look up your current and past colleagues' profiles on LinkedIn. You can so this by selecting the "Network" Tab and the sub page under this heading called "Find Alumni". Here, you will see all the people that you have listed on your profile, as well as how many people from your school are already LinkedIn members.

This will show you where these people live, where they work and what they do. You will get a list of people down below. Select the people you know.

Here you will see that you can either send them a message or connect with them. Now fill your network with new connections that are valuable.

LinkedIn is a great tool to find new customers, suppliers, partnerships, experts, and other people that would be valuable to add to your network. LinkedIn offers several ways to find specific types of people. But before being able to use LinkedIn successfully, it is important to create a good definition of your target group(s). Once you have defined your targets, here are some strategies to help you find them:

1.Browse the networks of your immediate network

You can do this by visiting someone's profile and looking at their connections on the right-hand side. If you see someone interesting, invite that person to connect.

2. Use the "advanced search" option to search for people

If you find someone with whom you'd like to connect, see if you share any mutual connections. Ask that connection if he or she can make an introduction to the new person. Please remember that what you are now doing is building a relationship. Don't sell at this stage.

3. Join groups that your target market joins

This will give you a genuine opportunity to interact with individuals of those groups and will help you increase your visibility. People will start to contact you.

4. Save your people searches and create an alert

If you set up an alert, LinkedIn will send you an email every week with new prospects. To do this, click on the blue search icon beside the search bar, click on "Save Search" this is located at the top right hand side of the screen, a box will open up where you can enter the "Search Name" and how often you want the alert sent to you, the options are "Never, Weekly, or Monthly". Don't forget to save!

5. Follow your network's updates and your contacts' interactions

As you watch who your network interacts with, you might notice opportunities for building valuable relationships. If someone mentions someone interesting, ask for an introduction.

LinkedIn is a very powerful tool to help you meet new contacts, grow your business network, and advance your career. Let's now dig into some of the specific business objectives you can reach.

How to Position Yourself in Your Industry

"We generate fears while we sit. We over come them by action. Fear is natures way of warning us to get busy" - Dr. Henry Link

Your main objective is to position yourself as a leader within your business or niche. You should also consider what your goal is as well. Is it to find customers and/or potential business partners? Or is your primary goal lead generation?

By determining who your target audience is you can then provide them with suitable content. This can be in the form of reports, articles, eBooks and even videos.

Remember that you should target your competition as well as other business associates. By sharing your information in this manner you will be seen as a force to be reckoned with. You could very easily have knowledge on one certain key aspect that even your competitor appreciates!

Other content that you could share with these people are the current and upcoming trends for your industry. Write a blog post on your thoughts and expectations and then sharing it with your connections.

The content that you share doesn't necessarily have to be yours 100% of the time. It is a great idea to share content from others in your industry, along with notes on your thoughts of how this service or product might affect your business.

The result of this over time will be that you are looked at as a leader in your industry. This is exactly what you want to have happen!

If you find that you are receiving good feedback from your connections then you should act on this and provide them with a free webinar or seminar. This can easily be set up online or offline depending upon your market.

As you become recognised as a leader you may wish to separate your website so that you have two focused sites. One site would be focused on your customers and their needs and wishes.

While the other would define you as a business leader and can possibly lead to speaking engagements or coaching clients.

How to use LinkedIn to Market Yourself

"Live daringly, boldly, fearlessly. Taste the relish to be found in competition - in having put forth the best within you" - Henry J. Kaiser

There are many objectives and goals that individuals have in how to market themselves. There are a variety of tools that we can all use on LinkedIn. These tools are beneficial if you are looking to become influential in your market, looking to get more leads, drive traffic to your website, want to sell more products, find that awesome job, build on your brand, find more clients, or sell tickets to an event you are running. Below is an overview of what you should be taking advantage of when you are marketing yourself on LinkedIn.

1. Give before asking for favors

This is important to do on any social networking site, but it's particularly important to do on LinkedIn when so many people are focused on receiving something for themselves or their business. The best way to give to others would be to make recommendations.

People are asking for recommendations all the time, when they haven't written any for others first. The more you recommend others without asking for one in return, the more it will give them a refreshing feeling about you and the more they'll want to be helpful in return.

Making introductions is also a great way to give. If you are trying to make a name for yourself, connect two people who you think could help each other build their businesses and achieve their goals.

2. Connect with everyone

It pains me to see when people only have fewer than 100 connections, and they think that having a "small trusted network" is the way to go.

That's a joke, and those with that mind set are going to be asking themselves why their message isn't spreading to the world and why they haven't achieved their marketing goals yet.

You never know where an opportunity or big breakthrough can come from. If you only share ideas with those you know and don't branch out to connect with new people, then you will only know about a limited amount of opportunities, and the same people who you talk to on a daily basis will be helping you connect with the same limited network. It's a never-ending circle of limitations, and it's time you break through that mind set if you haven't already.

Start adding your personal LinkedIn link to your email signature, on other social networking sites, on your business cards, and anywhere else you think would help inspire others to connect with you. Once you start receiving 10-20 inbound invitations to connect on a daily basis, then you know you're doing a good job marketing yourself.

3. Make your interactions personal

In general, people love human interaction. We don't want to connect with a business; we want to have relationships with others who we know, like, and trust. Every time you send an invitation to connect with someone, make it personal. Take out anything generic, and make it as personal as possible. That way the person will remember who you are, and will be more likely to follow up with you if you contact that person in the future.

Your profile should also include a personal element. Instead of making it look like a boring resume with a bunch of bullet point achievements, share your personal voice.

Tell people who you are and who you help. Place this information throughout your headline, summary, and the rest of your profile. Adding this will make others want to connect with you instead of putting them to sleep with your boring resume.

4..Create a call-to-action

People need to be led in the right direction that helps you achieve your goals. You can't just expect people to come to your LinkedIn profile and learn about some of things you do without telling them what to do next. If you don't create a call-to-action, then you are guaranteed to get less than what you desire. One way to create a call-to-action is by customising your website links.

LinkedIn lets you post three links, and instead of having them say "my blog," make it say "Contact Me Here" or "Download My Free Report." The more direct you can be, the better. Also, in your summary, after you tell people who you are, who you help, and how you can help them, tell them how they can and should get in touch with you. Whatever your goal, tell them to contact you or do something in a way that best meets your needs.

USING LINKEDIN ADVERTISING

"Sometimes when you innovate, you make mistakes. It is best to admit them quickly and get on with improving your other innovations" - Steve Jobs

You will find information about advertising on LinkedIn under the **Premium Solutions** tab of the navigation bar on your main page.

Anyone with a free account can use this service, but please note that it is a paid service.

A LinkedIn ad is an advertisement that functions as a self-service type of solution for business owners or job seekers. Your ads are displayed on prominent pages with LinkedIn.

You may target your ad by the following requirements:

- Job title
- Job function
- Industry
- Geography
- Age
- Gender
- Company name
- Company size
- LinkedIn group

You may control the money you spend on advertising by setting your own budget and paying for clicks or impressions.

Your ad will be displayed in a block containing other ads from members of LinkedIn.

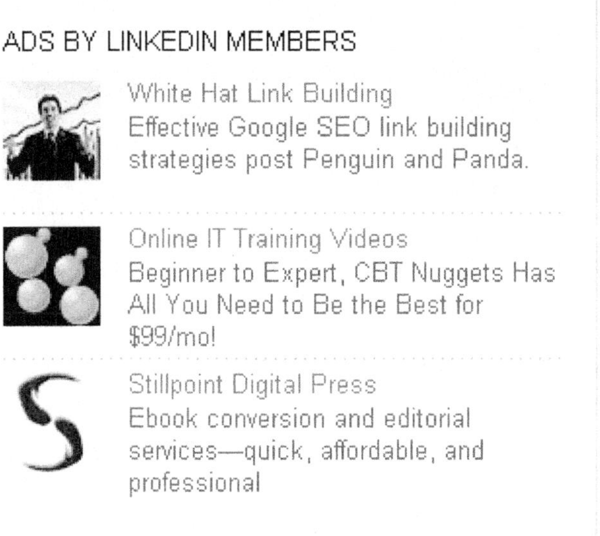

An advertisement on LinkedIn is constructed as follows:

- Headline: up to 25 characters of text
- Description: up to 75 characters of text
- From: Company or personal name
- Image: 50 x 50 pixels
- URL: website address you want to take people to

The most prominent places where you ads will be displayed are:

- Profile Pages
- Home Pages
- Inbox
- Search Results Page
- Groups

You must provide LinkedIn with a credit card account in order to use the LinkedIn ads feature. You may set your budget as low as $10 per day. Plus you can pause and re-start your ads whenever you wish.

YOUR LINKEDIN PROFILE BADGE

"The new source of power is not money in the hands of a few, but information in the hands of many" – John Naisbitt

Now that you have taken the time and effort to set up your LinkedIn account you want to make use of your **Profile Badge**. This can be found by clicking on the "edit your profile" button and then clicking on "Edit your public profile". On the bottom right hand side you will see a link for Profile Badges. Click on this and then select which type of badge you would like to use.

You can then add the code into your website or blog and make it very easy for your readers and customers to connect with you on LinkedIn.

You can also add this image to your email account if you wish.

First copy the code for the image you wish to use and save it to a notepad file.

You only want to use the actual image address, so copy from the http:// section to the end of png. This is the URL you will add to your signature.

For Gmail users simply go to your account setting and then click on the signature settings box.

1. Click on insert image
2. Insert the URL from your notepad file
3. If it is correct, the image will automatically appear in the box below.
4. Then click okay
5. Click on the image and then the hyperlink button
6. Add your LinkedIn profile address
7. Test the link and it should open directly to your profile page
8. Save changes and your LinkedIn badge now appears in your signature file

Now each time you send an email you are getting exposure to your LinkedIn account.

CONCLUSION

"Do or do not. There is no try" - Yoda

I truly hope that you enjoyed the training in this book and that it has given you valuable insights as to just what the new face of LinkedIn looks like.

LinkedIn has put a lot of time and effort into updating their site. Plus they waited until they were well established before making any major updates.

The new profile page allows everyone to view someone's profile in a professional manner. The site looks up to date and modern. The design was done to allow users to showcase and highlight their areas of expertise easily.

LinkedIn also provides helpful insights about your profile. This allows you to discover people who may be outside of your network and connect with them. By finding out what you have in common with others, you can easily make a better connection that is more likely to be accepted by the other person.

The **recent activity tab** allows you to quickly see what has been going on in your network each time you log in.

The improved **home page** lets you add links to either your recent articles that you have written, or to ones that you want to share with others in your network. All of these features and improvements have allowed LinkedIn to come out of the closet and emerge as a modern social site to be reckoned with.

Thanks and Good Luck!

About The Author

Sue Kennedy is an author and consultant.

Sydney Web Consultants is all about helping businesses utilise the Internet with effective online marketing strategies that will allow you to create a web presence so your business can grow and prosper. All facets of Online Marketing strategies are a vital tool for your business if you want to succeed. The future lies with the Internet; so being able to market your business effectively with online marketing strategies is an essential tool for your business. We have various services available to suit your individual requirements.

It is important to remember that online advertising is what works today and will continue to grow in the future. Do you want your business to get left behind or will you take the essential step and move forward with today's technology? A smart business decision is to invest in a strategic online marketing consultant to take care of all your online needs, and this is where Sydney Web Consultants can help you and your business.

Our Expertise

- Complete Market & Website Analysis - holistic & comprehensive
- Expertise – developed over 700 websites in every niche
- 20+ years combined "real world" business experience

Our Approach

- We help business owners gain more customers and sales. Plain and simple.
- The ways we do that are unique to each client. Even two clients in the same industry but different markets will be handled differently.
- Competitive analysis, market analysis, niche analysis, and analysis of each client's assets and collaterals
- We specialize in Search Engine Optimization and Web Marketing (Video, Articles, Press Releases, etc.)
- We offer clear benefits for your bottom line

- We can make your site Search Engine Friendly, Mobile Ready and Super-Easy to Update
- We offer no hard pitches, hype nor tricks...

Just Two Questions:

1. ***What do you want your online business to accomplish?***
2. ***In your market, what's the best way to achieve that?***

Only 2% of Your Market May Know Who You Are

Imagine Your Profits After the 98% Catches On!

Services Provided:

- Web Design and Development
- Custom Facebook Fan Pages
- Facebook Applications
- Copywriting & Sales Pages, Squeeze (Landing) Pages
- Mobile Marketing
- On-Page SEO
- Off-Page SEO
- Mobile Websites
- Mobile Applications
- Article Writing for your website or blog
- Press Releases
- Keyword Research Reports
- Video Creation and Marketing
- Google Places Local Listings
- Social Media Management
- Content Creation

If the service you are after is not listed above, please do not hesitate to contact us and ask – it is more likely than not that we can help

Offices in Sydney, Australia and Los Angeles, U.S.

Online Success in Business is Connecting Your Market to Your Website

How Can We Help You?

Sue@SydneyWebConsultants.com.au

1300 36 77 27

SydneyWeb Consultants
Recession-Proof Marketing

www.SydneyWebConsultants.com.au

LET'S GET CONNECTED!!
LINK & GROW YOUR BUSINESS ON LINKEDIN

NOTES

NOTES

Printed in Dunstable, United Kingdom

91219599R00060